A colour atlas of
Ophthalmological
Diagnosis

Second edition

M. A. Bedford
FRCS
Honorary Consulting Surgeon,
Moorfields Eye Hospital,
lately Consultant-in-Charge,
Eye Department,
St Bartholomew's Hospital, London

Wolfe Medical Publications Ltd

NHS Staff Library at St James's

To renew this book please phone 0113 20 65638, or e-mail lthstafflibraries@nhs.net. You can also renew this book online using the NHS Library Catalogue. Please ask library staff for details.

The Leeds Teaching Hospitals
NHS Trust

Diagnosis

General Editor, Wolfe Medical Books
G. Barry Carruthers MD (Lond)

This book is one of the titles in the series of Wolfe
Medical Atlases, a series which brings together
probably the world's largest systematic published
collection of diagnostic colour photographs.

For a full list of Atlases in the series, plus
forthcoming titles and details of our surgical, dental
and veterinary Atlases, please write to Wolfe
Medical Publications Ltd, Brook House,
2-16 Torrington Place, London WC1E 7LT.

Contents

		Page
Introduction		6
PART 1		
Methods of examination		7
PART 2		
The red eye		39
PART 3		
Loss of vision in a white eye		59
a) Gradual		60
b) Sudden		80
PART 4		
Eye injuries		85
a) Minor		86
b) Major		98
PART 5		
Miscellaneous		121
a) Common conditions		122
b) Less common conditions		146
Index		181

Introduction

This work is intended to be an atlas, not a textbook. No attempt is made to cover the whole field of ophthalmology. The book is aimed at the hard-pressed undergraduate or family doctor who has not the time (or the inclination) to delve deeply into a textbook containing optical theory and obscure pathological conditions surrounded by complicated ocular terms unlike any others encountered in the rest of medicine.

In the first chapter emphasis is placed on a practical examination, which is described step by step and which can be carried out with a minimum of simple instrumentation by someone not necessarily skilled in ophthalmology. In addition, there are short descriptions of diagnostic instruments an eye surgeon may use.

This is followed by chapters dealing with the evaluation of common clinical patterns that the non-ophthalmologist may be confronted with: for example, the red eye, loss of vision in an apparently normal-looking white eye, eye injuries, and so on. In each of these chapters an attempt is made to show how the diagnosis can be made using the method of examination described in Part 1.

It is hoped that this atlas will help the average medical man to sort out ocular problems, which might well otherwise defeat him.

Acknowledgements

My publisher has demonstrated the need for this second edition. New photographs have been added and the text altered. Thanks are due to my colleagues who have aided me. Many of the photographs of 'old-fashioned' techniques, e.g. Schiøtz tonometry, peripheral fields, etc., have been retained because these are the only techniques available in some countries. Sadly, the politics and industrialisation of the 1980s have demonstrated the need to retain conditions such as mustard gas keratitis and penetrating eye injuries, which one would have hoped could have been deleted. Finally, thanks to my wife for her help, criticism and typing ability.

M. A. BEDFORD
1986

PART 1

Methods of examination:

Estimation of visual acuity   8

Examination of the outside of the eye   10

Examination of the inside of the eye   20

Other tests not used routinely:

Assessment of intra-ocular pressure   28

Assessment of visual fields   32

Estimation of visual acuity

1 When confronted with a patient complaining of an ocular disorder of any sort, the first point to establish is: what can the patient actually see? This is estimated with the well known Snellen test chart, which should be used at a distance of 6 metres from the patient. This '6' is the top number of the fraction 6/6, which is normal visual acuity. On the figure opposite, this is the ability to read the third line from the bottom. The lowest two lines are necessary because very often the patient's visual acuity can be better than normal, i.e. 6/5 (able to read the second line from the bottom) or 6/4 (able to read the bottom line). The reasoning behind this chart is that, taking the top letter, the normal person can see this at 60 metres as it subtends ten times the angle of the letters on the 6/6 line. Similarly, a normal person can see the second line, O E, at 36 metres and the lines underneath at 24, 18, 12 and 9 metres. If testing at 6 metres and the patient can see only the second line from the top (O E) the vision is thus 6/36.

There are several points to bear in mind when testing the visual acuity: do not waste time doing binocular visual acuity, but test one eye at a time and always test the eye the patient is not complaining about first, as this can be a very useful control.

The approximate equivalents to Snellen's notation in feet and in the decimal system are:

Snellen's notation		Decimal notation
Metres	Feet	
6/6	20/20	1·0
6/9	20/30	0·7
6/12	20/40	0·5
6/18	20/60	0·3
6/24	20/80	0·25
6/60	20/200	0·1

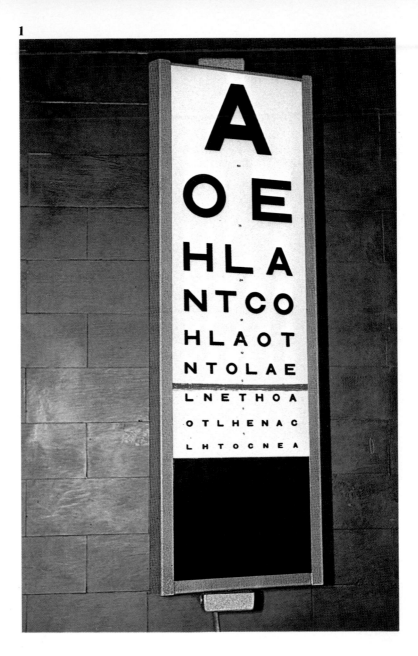

1

2 Always use an opaque card to occlude the other eye. If you use your own hand or the patient's hand there may be small gaps between the fingers, through which the patient may sometimes look, thus giving a false reading. The card can be easily moved across to the other eye; there is thus no doubt as to the separate visual acuity of each eye. Naturally, the tests should be done with the patient wearing his distance glasses or bifocals. This is a point well worth remembering, for to save time the patient, knowing that he is to see the doctor about his eyes, will tend to remove his glasses before coming in for the examination.

Examination of the outside of the eye

3 Next consider the examination proper, taking it in a logical order. First, examine the outside of the eye. This is best done by using an ordinary hand light and holding up the upper lid as shown. Points to be noticed are: is the eye white or red? Are the pupils reacting normally? Is there a nice bright corneal reflex? This last is a sight that pleases all eye surgeons, for it proves that the essential transparent window of the eye (the cornea) is probably normal, if the highlight shown by the reflection of the examiner's hand light is bright and clearly defined.

2

3

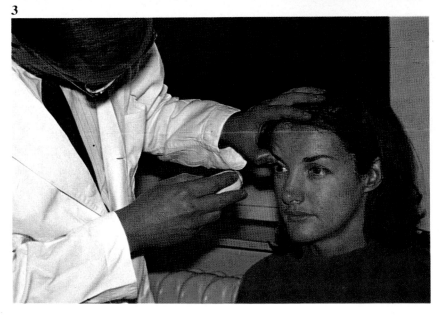

4 & 4a The patient should be instructed to look to the right, to the left, up and down. Both eyes should be examined in this way. It is impossible to see the deep aspect of the upper lid without a further manoeuvre termed 'eversion' (**5**).

4

4a

13

5 It may be necessary to evert the upper lid, particularly if the patient is complaining of, say, a foreign body that has not so far become apparent in the routine examination. The best method is to stand behind the patient as shown. When everting the right upper lid, the doctor should pull the lid out with his right hand, then turn the lid over the index finger of his left hand.

6 The lid is now everted and any foreign body present is easily removed. Such movements, of course, should be reversed for the eversion of the left upper lid. If the foreign body has been present for some time, whenever the patient has blinked a linear corneal ulcer will have been formed. These ulcers may be very severe; their size may be estimated by applying fluorescein (**7**).

5

6

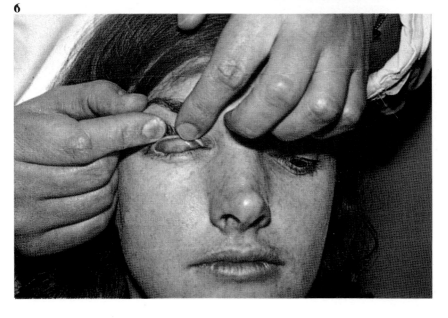

7 The application of fluorescein is essential in making the diagnosis of loss of epithelium on a transparent structure like the cornea, for otherwise it is impossible to see with the naked eye. Nowadays, fluorescein is supplied in two main ways: either as a sterile single-dose container (top left) containing a small quantity of fluorescein eye drops; or as a small piece of filter paper impregnated with fluorescein at one end. These are available in sterile containers (bottom right) and are easily removed for use (centre). All that is necessary is to apply a minute trace of fluorescein by either method to the outside corner of the eye, and then irrigate any excess away. An ulcer, if present, will be visible as a brilliant green area (**7a**).

7

7a

8 We have seen from the foregoing exposition how the general practitioner, with his limited resources, may examine the outside of the eye. However, the eye surgeon has more sophisticated equipment: he can, for instance, work with the instrument shown here to look at the anterior half of the eye under magnification. This instrument is a slit-lamp, basically a microscope mounted slightly obliquely to a very thin beam of light, which can give an optical section of the front half of the eye, as shown in **9**.

9 On the left is the curved beam of light striking the cornea and passing over towards the right into the anterior chamber of the eye, striking the iris and the lens. In the anterior chamber are some white spots, which are aggregations of cells denoting inflammatory pathology inside the eye. This instrument is essential in the management of all serious eye diseases.

8

9

Examination of the inside of the eye

10 The inside of the eye should now be examined with the ophthalmoscope. Valuable information, however, may be gained by keeping a foot away from the patient and looking through the ophthalmoscope as shown here. Note that the clinician is examining the **right** eye of the patient, using his **right** eye with the ophthalmoscope in his **right** hand.

11 This view may be seen through the ophthalmoscope using this manoeuvre in the normal eye. There is the normal **'red reflex'** as it is termed — and remember that it is red because the light is being reflected back from the choroid, the overlying retina being virtually transparent. It means that a) there must be transparent media in front of the retina, and b) the retina is adposed to the choroid. Thus any loss of the red reflex means that there is either i) an opacity in the media preventing the light from going through, or ii) the retina is not against the choroid and is out of position. In terms of pathology there is one of three conditions: a cataract, a vitreous haemorrhage, or a retinal detachment.

10

11

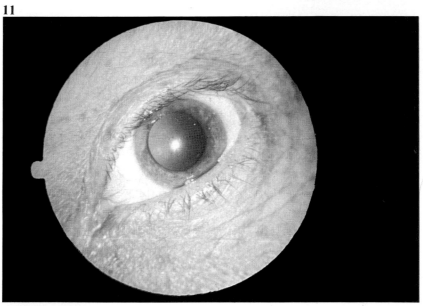

12 Note that here there is no red reflex, but a rather characteristic greyness, which suggests that there is a total retinal detachment. A similar loss of red reflex, particularly associated with an opacity that can be seen anteriorly while using the hand light in the examination of the outside of the eye, would mean that a cataract is present. Having seen the normal red reflex, the examiner should then move his head and ophthalmoscope near to the patient — and emphasis is placed on the **nearness.**

13 Note that the examiner's forehead is actually touching the patient's forehead. This is logical — to look at the view from a window, one gets as close to the window as possible. There is no other way of examining the inside of the eye properly than to get as **close as possible,** and for this reason the examiner uses his **right** eye with the ophthalmoscope in his **right** hand when looking at the **right** eye of the patient, and reverses all these manoeuvres when examining the left eye. It is impossible to examine a patient's fundus if both the examiner and the patient are standing up: one cannot get close enough.

12

13

14 The view of the normal fundus as seen with the ophthalmoscope. The following points should be noted:

a) **The disc** — its colour, its cup and its margins. Note the healthy pink colour, the central white depression, which is the cup, and the well-defined margins.

b) **The vessels** — note their calibre and their crossing, then look at the general **background colour** of the fundus, which may vary and should be correlated with the colouring and race of the patient.

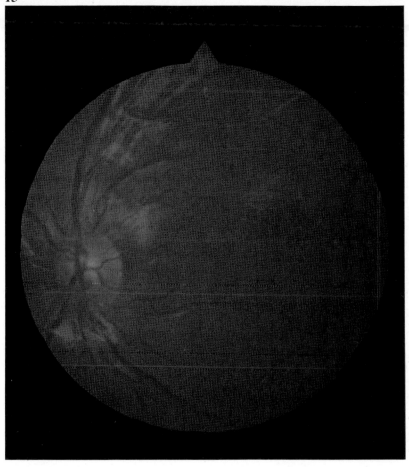

15 A dark fundus, which may be seen in a negro person. The fine white lines are light reflections from the retinal fibres.

16 A typical myopic albinoid fundus showing the myopic 'crescent' around the disc and the general thinning of the retina and choroid, the choroidal vessels showing through as flat ribbons because of the small amount of pigment epithelium present beneath the retina. Through the undilated pupil only the disc and paramacular area may be seen, and at this point if one's suspicions are aroused the pupils may be dilated. A short-acting mydriatic (pupil-dilating) drop should be used such as cyclopentolate, tropicamide or hyoscine — never atropine, because its action lasts for 10 to 14 days.

Assessment of intra-ocular pressure

17 If necessary, and particularly if the diagnostic problem of acute glaucoma has been raised, it will be essential to assess the intra-ocular pressure. This is done by **digital palpation** as shown here. Note that both hands rest on the patient's forehead; one would assess the normal eye first and then the eye under suspicion. Most examiners will probably never pick up the slight elevation in both eyes in chronic simple glaucoma (**57 & 58**), but relatively unskilled observers can easily pick up the very high pressure characteristic of an acute glaucoma (**33 to 35**) in one eye. A discrepancy is only too obvious if the normal eye is palpated first.

18 The classical way of measuring the intra-ocular pressure as practised in eye hospitals is with the **Schiøtz tonometer.** Below can be seen a small plunger about to rest on the anaesthetised cornea; obviously, the degree that the plunger moves down governs the sweep of the pointer above. This is not very accurate and another technique is used in modern eye departments, as shown in **19**.

17

18

19 This is a little prism mounted on the slit-lamp, which is rested delicately on the front of the cornea. The amount of force used to produce a standard deformation is measured and this gives an index of the pressure (**applanation tonometry**). This is probably the most accurate method of measuring the intra-ocular pressure at present.

20 If necessary, the state of the tear passages may be assessed by syringing them. The patient may feel the water running into his nose if the passages are clear. This is a manoeuvre that can be done by medical practitioners but it is time-consuming, needs a special cannula, and in most cases is probably best done by the surgeon in hospital.

19

20

Assessment of visual fields

21 If necessary, the other aspect of visual function, i.e. the visual fields, may be assessed. These need not be estimated in every case as the tests are time-consuming: they should be reserved for the problem of the patient who has had difficulty in seeing with optimum spectacle lenses, and where there is no ocular pathology yet noted in the examination, or perhaps a suspicion of optic atrophy has been seen with the ophthalmoscope. Visual fields are easily assessed by **confrontation,** but note that the examiner's hand is covering the eye that is not being examined, and the patient's other eye is being fixed by the examiner's opposite eye to make sure that the point of fixation does not move. In addition, note that the examiner has closed his own eye — the one corresponding to the covered eye of the patient — i.e. the examiner is comparing the patient's visual field with his own. The examiner's free hand is exactly halfway between them. Such a method of examination is very rough; if a defect is picked up it should be examined in detail on a machine such as that shown in the next figure (**22**).

22 The patient is maintaining her gaze on the central white spot while a nurse is rotating a handle at the back of the machine, which moves the peripheral white spot; as this moves inwards the patient signifies when she first sees it. Although this method is old-fashioned, it is very reliable and inexpensive and is still used in many parts of the world.

21

22

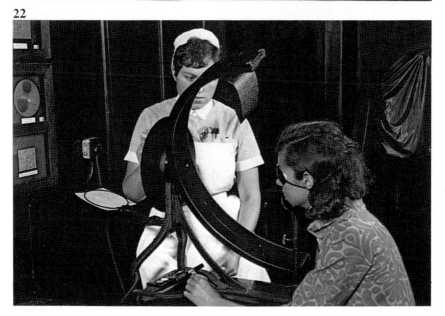

23 There is a metal spike on the back of the machine that is geared to move with the white spot actuated by the nurse, who merely moves the card up and punches a hole in it at the appropriate moment.

24 The **peripheral field** here seen on the right is of course of one eye and is restricted above and nasally. This is the right peripheral field and the restrictions are caused by the brow and nose. The defect seen, as marked by red ink, is a temporal hemianopia and, if present in both eyes, would signify a pituitary tumour. Unfortunately, pituitary tumours can produce not peripheral field defects, as noted here, but **central field** defects and the larger chart shown on the left corresponds to only 30° from the central point of vision. It is a very magnified area of the centre of the peripheral field chart. A field defect can occur just within a few degrees of fixation and can have the same sinister significance as a larger peripheral field defect. This sort of central field scotoma will not be picked up by the perimeter and has to be done in a special way.

SCOTOMA CHART
for use with
GREEVE'S PORTABLE
BJERRUM SCREEN

NAME
VISION

DATE
Scale 3 mm.—1°

Keeler

RIGHT EYE
ONLY

R

LOCATE

HAMBLIN
PERIMETER
& SCOTOMETER
CHART

Published by THEODORE HAMBLIN LTD

25 The examiner is dressed in black so as not to distract the patient's fixation. He holds a wand terminating in a white spot and the patient signifies whether she can see it or not as it is moved around. The examiner then inserts a series of small pins on the screen to map out the blind spots, when present. Such a test is time-consuming, but is probably one of the most accurate methods of doing a central visual field. It is also very cheap and is thus easily used in any part of the world.

26 This shows a modern machine whereby an observer can move a light, which can be controlled both in intensity and size, around the inside of a concave bowl. The patient, whose head is immobilized, signifies when the object moves into his field of vision (one eye being done at a time). It is then recorded on the back of the machine, the net result being a combination of central and peripheral fields under extremely standardised conditions. It is probably an ideal method, but the machine is very expensive. (Illustration courtesy of Clement Clarke Ltd.)

25

26

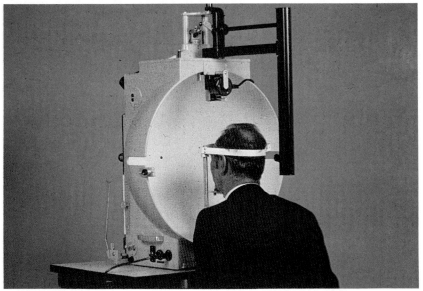

Although some of the steps shown here should clearly be undertaken by a special examiner with special equipment, e.g. use of the slit-lamp and tonometer, and assessment of peripheral and central fields, the salient points of the examination can be achieved with three simple instruments:

a) The **visual acuity chart** to determine the visual function.

b) The **hand light** to examine the outside of the eye.

c) The **ophthalmoscope** to examine the inside of the eye.

In the following chapters this method of examination will be emphasised when sorting out the diagnosis of the red eye or loss of vision in a white eye, etc., as it can be easily practised almost anywhere.

PART 2

The red eye

This chapter is concerned with sorting out what is probably the most common ophthalmological problem seen by the family doctor — the 'red eye'. Emphasis will be placed on the method of examination previously described and each illustration will be discussed as if it is of the patient that the doctor is actually examining.

Blepharitis   40

Conjunctivitis   42

Iridocyclitis   45

Acute glaucoma   50

Non-traumatic corneal ulcers   54

These conditions will be diagnosed primarily by examining the outside of the eye, as shown in figures **3 to 7.**

27 & 27a This patient is complaining of sore red eyes or red eye-lids, which have been present perhaps for some months. He may complain of itching, irritation or soreness, the element of pain being small, and the symptoms being more of a trivial nature but very persistent and worrying.

On examination, his visual acuity is normal; the outside of his eye examined with a hand light shows the physical signs seen in the illustrations, and the inside of the eye is normal on examination with the ophthalmoscope. It will be seen that the eye is white, or it may be slightly congested, and there is a nice bright corneal reflex, the pupils reacting briskly. The only relevant physical signs are **red and thickening eye-lids** with some **scaling** along the margins. This is termed **blepharitis.** The condition is essentially infective in nature, but there is little point in giving eye drops to be instilled in the conjunctival sac as this is not primarily involved in the pathology. A clue to the precise pathology can be seen on examination of the eye-lashes, when it is noticed that they may be missing or, as in these cases, perhaps deformed and not pointing in their true direction. The infection is thus in the follicle of the lash and any treatment given must be aimed at this site. Useful treatment is for the patient to apply an antibiotic eye ointment by putting it on his little finger and then rubbing it into the roots of the eye-lashes night and morning. This will enable the scales to be removed and the antibiotic to reach down into the follicles. Treatment may take many weeks or months and in some cases the condition is almost impossible to cure. It is almost always bilateral, but can be asymmetrical.

27

27a

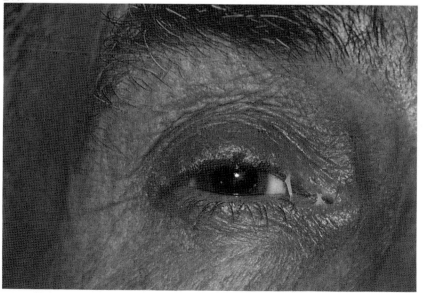

28 & 28a This patient may state that his eyes are sore and red and have been so for several days. On examination, his visual acuity is normal, and the outside of his eye shows the physical signs illustrated here, **congestion being present on the back of the lids and on the membrane reflected upwards from the lower fornix to the limbus** (that is the line of junction where the transparent window of the eye, the cornea, fuses with the white protective sclera and the conjunctiva). There is only one structure continuous on the lid and the globe and that is the conjunctiva, so this is a **conjunctivitis** and, classically, the congestion is less adjacent to the limbus, for the conjunctiva is thinner there.

Conjunctivitis may be defined as an acute inflammatory condition, usually viral or bacterial in nature. In the busy general practice this is of academic importance, for certainly most cases will never be cultured. The classical signs and symptoms are a feeling of **soreness or grittiness;** pain is not usually predominant; the eyes are **red and congested;** it is **bilateral but can be asymmetrical** as one would expect from an infective condition. The visual acuity is of course unaffected, as the essential seeing mechanism of the eye is not involved in the inflammation. However, at times some discharge may collect over the cornea, which disturbs vision, but this is cleared by blinking and is thus only momentary in nature. One of the classical symptoms is that the patient's eye-lids stick together overnight, as the secretions dry at the lid margins.

Treatment is vigorous and usually means application of a suitable antibiotic drop with an antibiotic ointment at night. Should the condition not respond in 7 to 10 days, the diagnosis should be reconsidered. **Never make a diagnosis of monocular conjunctivitis.** In view of the definition stated, it presupposes that a monocular conjunctivitis is not infective, i.e. it must be secondary to other pathology, for example a missed foreign body, or blocked tear passages, or, more likely, it may not be conjunctivitis at all.

28

28a

29 Occasionally, systemic conditions present with a conjunctivitis that does not respond fully to conventional means. Here is the lower conjunctival sac of a patient complaining of a sore red eye that persisted in spite of antibiotic drops. Closer examination reveals a small gelatinous nodule, which on biopsy showed the classical appearances of sarcoidosis.

30 Note the type of congestion demonstrated by this photograph. **The redness is maximal adjacent to the limbus and grows less** as it spreads to the fornices to the back of the lid. Clearly, this is the reverse of the congestion of a conjunctivitis; an eye showing this sort of congestion should be examined with extreme caution as it is highly likely that the essential seeing mechanism inside the eye is involved in an inflammatory process of one sort or another.

31 & 31a This patient complains of a sore red eye with a loss of vision lasting for several days. It may be bilateral but is usually unilateral. On examination the visual acuity shows perhaps a slight loss, it may be 6/18 or 6/12. It is difficult to see the inside of the eye because of the haze situated anteriorly within the globe.

The first point to notice is that the **pupil is irregular** and the general details of the iris are rather hazy. The congestion does **not** involve the back of the lids. The haze must be caused by pathology anterior to the iris and there are only two structures here. They are a) the outermost transparent cornea and b) the aqueous separating the cornea from the iris. Note that there is a nice bright corneal reflex present, showing that the cornea is normal, so the essential haze is between the cornea and the iris – that is, in the anterior chamber. Correlating this with an acute red eye, this must mean an inflammatory exudate, showing that this is a case of an **acute iridocyclitis,** or inflammation of the iris and ciliary body. The physical signs may be built up by applying the principles of inflammation as can be seen in the rest of the body. Clearly, there will be swelling and the iris swells in all dimensions, in width and thickness, so that the pupil will be small and slightly sticky because of the inflammatory exudate within it and around it. As it is sticky, the pupillary margin adheres to the lens and sticks in the points seen in the figure, which are termed 'posterior synechiae'. These may become permanent (**31a**).

If the exudate is severe enough, the aggregations of cells may be seen as minute white spots in the centre of the pupil (see **31**). These are classically adherent to the back of the cornea and are termed keratic precipitates (KP). The patient is best referred to an eye specialist, as the condition may not be an isolated intra-ocular inflammation but part of a general systemic disease that may require further investigation, e.g. a collagen disease, auto-immune disease, some venereal diseases, ankylosing spondylitis, diabetes, Reiter's syndrome, etc.

31

31a

32 In early cases, if the pupil can be fully dilated, the aggregates of cells may be seen against the red reflex of the fundus by using an ophthalmoscope, as seen here (or by the slit-lamp used by the eye-surgeon).

In summary, then, **acute iridocyclitis** is an inflammatory but not infective process of the iris and ciliary body characterised by a **red eye, visual loss and a small, sticky pupil.** Treatment is to dilate the pupil with atropine, homatropine or hyoscine and to suppress the inflammation with either systemic or local steroids.

33 This patient complains of a sudden severe loss of vision, perhaps preceded by haloes around lights and pain that may be appalling – he may vomit and even collapse. On examination, the visual acuity may be less than 6/60 and examination of the outside of his eye shows there is a haze anterior to the iris: because of this haze examination of the inside of the eye with the ophthalmoscope is impossible. The same reasoning should now apply as in the previous case of acute iridocyclitis, when the iris was also obscured by a haze. However, note that in this case the bright corneal reflex is lacking, so the haze must be caused by a disturbance of the cornea. This disturbance is **corneal oedema** and is pathognomonic of an **acute glaucoma** — an acute rise in intra-ocular pressure (the increased pressure forces fluid into the cornea giving rise to the oedema). Note that because the seeing mechanism of the eye is involved, **congestion is limbal** in nature, i.e. maximal at the junction of the cornea and sclera and conjunctiva. The pressure may rise so high that there is pressure necrosis of the sphincter and the pupil becomes dilated and fixed.

34 A further case of acute glaucoma showing the severe corneal oedema and the classical limbal congestion. Note also that an attempt has been made at surgical treatment by removal of part of the iris.

35 Diagram showing the flow of aqueous from the ciliary body around the pupillary border, as shown by the red arrow, into the angle. The angle is adjacent to the circular canal of Schlemm, which runs around the limbus; the aqueous humour, after draining out here, passes into the subconjunctival plexus of blood vessels. There is a continuous flow of aqueous, and blockage in the angle will give rise to a precipitate increase in the intra-ocular pressure.

Eyes vary in their shape: there can be short, fat eyes and long, thin eyes. Acute glaucoma appears in rather short, fat eyes (hypermetropic or far-sighted) where the angles are 'crowded' to begin with. As the volume of the iris is constant it can be either long and thin (pupil small) or short and fat (pupil large) and when it is short and fat it may obstruct the angle and cause the intra-ocular pressure to rise. This is an ophthalmic emergency, and the pressure must be reduced as rapidly as possible by giving drops to make the pupil smaller, e.g. pilocarpine and eserine, thus freeing the angle. All cases should be admitted to hospital, as operation may be needed.

In summary, there is **severe pain and marked visual loss** with **corneal oedema** and classically an **oval, eccentric, dilated pupil.** Treatment is to make the pupil smaller. It must be reiterated that the treatments of acute iridocyclitis and acute glaucoma are exactly opposite.

36 There is one other condition that may appear as a painful red eye and that is an acute corneal ulcer. There are two forms of corneal ulcer: a) non-traumatic, and b) traumatic. The latter will be discussed in a later chapter.

Non-traumatic corneal ulcers are diagnosed by the instillation of fluorescein, as described in the methods of examination. The corneal ulcer will then be picked out as a green area of varying dimensions, as seen in the illustration. The patient complains of a sore, red eye, the visual acuity may be unaffected, and the clue that it is a corneal condition is given by the fact that there may be varying amounts of blepharospasm and lacrimation. Should this be noted, fluorescein should be immediately instilled and the ulcer will be seen: in this case the ulcer overlies the pupil.

37 The fluorescein can be made more obvious by using a cobalt blue light with the slit-lamp, as seen in this figure, demonstrating a non-traumatic corneal ulcer caused by the herpes simplex virus and termed a **dendritic ulcer,** as in **36**. The treatment of all corneal ulcers is to cover the eye with a pad and bandage, but it is probably best if these common non-traumatic ulcers are referred for specialist attention as they may progress and cause corneal scarring with loss of vision. In no circumstances must these patients be given local steroids, as this would facilitate the spread of herpes simplex virus and prevent healing. (See next case, **38**.)

38 This patient may give a history that she attended for treatment some weeks before with sore red eyes and that she was prescribed eyedrops. Her eyes then felt better, but now they suddenly feel worse. On examination, this characteristic picture is seen: the eye is congested, the white level is pus in the anterior chamber. This is termed a **hypopyon,** and although it may arise spontaneously in some conditions, it should be borne in mind that the patient may previously have been prescribed eyedrops that contained steroids, which would, of course, facilitate the growth of any organisms. It is dangerous to prescribe local steroids with or without an antibiotic unless adequate slit-lamp serial observation is made. Hypopyon ulcers are extremely serious, as the infection has only to pass into the vitreous jelly inside the eye and a pan-ophthalmitis will occur. Occasionally, a hypopyon may be seen as part of a systemic collagen disease. All cases of hypopyon should be referred for urgent specialist treatment.

37

38

39 Occasionally, a patient may complain of rather odd atypical symptoms with a sore, red eye. A valuable clue may be ascertained by examining the face of the patient, as in this case. This is a case of **herpes zoster ophthalmicus** and such a condition should always be referred for expert treatment, for apart from corneal ulceration, iridocyclitis, glaucoma, optic atrophy and retinal changes, the condition may result in chronic pain that may last for years.

Although the diagnosis is obvious in this patient, sometimes only a few vesicles may be present on the brow and nose. In all cases of red eyes it is well worth while to view the patient as a complete person initially, before becoming too involved with the local condition.

PART 3

Loss of vision in a white eye

There are many causes of loss of vision in an apparently normal-looking white eye. As the globe looks virtually normal from the outside we have to consider all structures posterior to the iris. The visual changes can be subdivided into a) gradual loss, and b) sudden loss. Then each of these subdivisions should be classified further on an anatomical basis, working posteriorly from the lens to the retina, the choroid, optic disc and optic nerves to the chiasm. In all these cases the patient has come to the doctor saying he is not seeing so well and it has come on either suddenly or gradually.

Gradual loss of vision

Cataract   60

Retinal changes
   Systemic diseases — Hypertension   66
                         Diabetes   68, 70
   Inflammation — Toxoplasmosis   72
                   Syphilis   72
   Papilloedema   74

Optic nerves
   Chronic glaucoma   76
   Atrophy   78

Sudden loss of vision

Retinal problems
   Vascular — Arterial block   80
               Venous block   80
   Detachment   82

These conditions will be diagnosed primarily by a) estimation of visual acuity (**1 & 2**), and b) examination of the inside of the eye (**10 to 16**).

Gradual loss of vision

40 This shows a complete opacity of the lens known as a **mature or ripe cataract.** The vision will be less than 6/60. On examination of the outside of the eye, the opacity appears white. However, with the ophthalmoscope no light enters the eye to be reflected back from the retina and choroid, so there is no red reflex — it appears completely black. This is true of all lens opacities: when looking at them they appear white, and when attempting to look through them they appear black or grey. Normally, cataracts are not allowed to remain unoperated on if they become too mature or too ripe as they may predispose to intra-ocular inflammation, glaucoma or sometimes dislocation (see **82**).

41 This illustration shows a row of minute white flecks concentric with the pupil when they are looked at with the hand light.

42 This illustration shows a row of opacities similar to those in **41**, which may be seen against the red reflex when using the ophthalmoscope. Cataracts may be classified as a) congenital, b) senile or c) acquired. The third group (acquired) is very large, as lens opacities may be considered as interferences in the lens metabolism of any sort, e.g. radiation, drugs, injury, etc. The opacity in the lens will develop only while the interference with metabolism is occurring: thus the localisation of the lens opacity and its shape may give a valuable clue as to the cause of the cataract.

43 Note a central lens opacity surrounded by clear lens through which the normal red reflex is seen. Clearly, interference to metabolism was occurring when the innermost earliest fibres were being laid down, so this is a type of **congenital cataract.**

44 A characteristic disc-shaped loss of red reflex situated in the posterior part of the lens characteristic of **radiation cataract.**

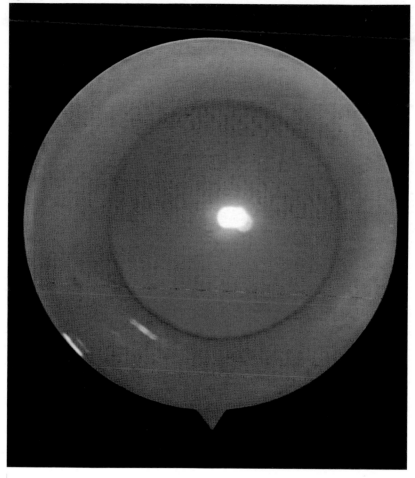

45 A few globules can be seen adjacent to the highlight of the examiner's light, caused by long-continued use of systemic steroids. This is an early **steroid cataract.**

46 Hypertensive retinopathy. Many patients with hypertension initially complain of visual changes, disregarding their other symptoms. There may be slight changes in visual acuity, the outside of the eyes may appear normal, but on the inside this fundus picture can be seen. Note the calibre and the crossing of the arteries over the veins. Haemorrhages may be seen, but the main changes are arterial (see **47 & 54**).

47 A florid hypertensive retinopathy. Note the arterial changes, i.e. the increased 'silver wire' reflections from the arteries with marked arteriovenous nipping.

46

47

48 A case of **diabetic retinopathy.** Note the vascular changes predominantly at the posterior pole of the eye, with micro-aneurysms and 'dot and blot' haemorrhages, together with hard exudates arranged side by side. There are minimal arteriovenous changes.

49 Many diseases, particularly of the auto-immune or collagen systems, can show a retinopathy. This is the retinopathy of lupus erythematosus. Notice the many soft white exudates.

48

49

50 This illustration shows new vessel formation towards the periphery of the globe typical of a form of diabetic retinopathy that can be slowed down by light-coagulation, as in **51** (same case).

51 The rounded yellowish speckled areas are the separate burns after light coagulation, which improve oxygenation of the inner surfaces of the retina, thus slowing down the neovascularisation.

50

51

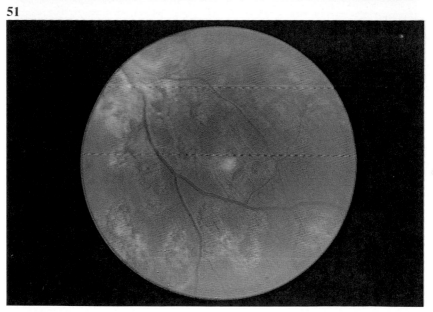

52 Toxoplasmosis choroidoretinitis. These cases commonly present later, with an active focus towards one edge of the lesion. Note the white scarring and the black proliferation of pigment: an area of active inflammation on this will present as an ill-defined, whitish opacity, the area being white because it is thicker, and thus less of the normal red reflex will be showing through. This is the most common cause of an acute focal choroidoretinitis.

53 Patches of disseminated choroidoretinitis, i.e. confluent rounded patches of scarring and proliferation of the pigment epithelium. Such a picture should immediately suggest syphilis.

52

53

54 Superimposed on a hypertensive retinopathy may be disc changes. Note the congested disc with the fine capillaries, particularly on the nasal side, with early swelling. This is early **papilloedema.**

55 A further stage of papilloedema. Note the gross swelling of the disc and the way the vessels tumble over the edge. Apart from this, note that there is relatively little vascular change with no retinopathy. This is the sort of swelling seen in benign intracranial hypertension.

54

55

56 A severe form of papilloedema. Note the obliterated disc margins, the gross swelling and the way the vessels tumble over the edge of the disc, the whole being surrounded by a ring of scattered haemorrhages. This gross form of papilloedema may be seen in renal hypertension or in tumours of the optic nerve or of the brain.

57 Early suspicious glaucomatous cup. Note that the cup is enlarged and the vessels dip over the edge. Such a disc, even in the absence of symptoms, should be referred for the assessment of **chronic glaucoma.** The visual acuity may be normal. This form of glaucoma (as opposed to acute glaucoma — the red eye) is insidious, there being no pain or redness, only a reduction of visual function extending over many months. The appearance of the optic disc gives the clue.

56

57

58 Early glaucomatous field. Note that on the left is the right normal central field with the blind spot. On the right is seen the classical **arcuate scotoma** as the blind spot extends up and over the point of fixation. This is caused by pressure on the optic nerve, which presses on the normal physiological cup, enlarges it and pushes it out of the eye. Such pressure can lead to almost complete blindness if it continues for years.

59 Optic atrophy. When a patient who is complaining of visual changes has normal physical signs at the front of the eye, but pale discs like this are noted, the fields should be examined by confrontation. Pituitary tumours, orbital tumours, the end result of disseminated sclerosis and spirochaetal disease, may all present with similar optic atrophy.

58

59

79

Sudden loss of vision

60 Blockage of the central retinal artery (lower branch). This patient complains of sudden loss of vision. After the outside of the eye is examined and appears normal, the inside shows this condition. Note the loss of red reflex below; instead there is a whitish colour. This is because the retina is thickened and less choroid shows through. The other important physical sign is that the artery is collapsed in that portion of the retina. The white area is thus a patch of ischaemic necrosis caused by a blockage of the artery supplying it. Sometimes the whole retinal artery will be blocked, so that the whole fundus presents this milky appearance and the ensuing visual loss is catastrophic and permanent. Causes are numerous, but the one that should first be considered is **temporal** or **giant cell arteritis,** particularly in the elderly. If the condition is not diagnosed, the other eye may well be affected and the patient made permanently blind. Other causes are hypertension, arteriosclerosis, emboli and collagen diseases.

61 Retinal vein thrombosis. The patient complains of a loss of vision, but not as dramatic or severe as in the previous case. The artery is still pumping blood into the eye and the obstruction may be partway along the vein (in this case the upper half), or sometimes at the disc. In either case the retina distal to the block is broken up by a sheet of haemorrhages extending from the point of obstruction.

60

61

62 Retinal detachment. This patient complains of sudden loss or change in vision, perhaps preceded by black spots or flashing lights. The retinal detachment is caused by a retinal hole; as the hole is forming the retina is irritated, giving flashing lights subjectively. The hole may tear across small capillaries, causing minor vitreous haemorrhages, and these are seen as black flies or cobwebs by the patient. The retina then detaches and hangs into the eye as a grey balloon. Such a localised loss of red reflex with this characteristic greyness should immediately lead to the diagnosis of retinal detachment. Treatment is urgent and requires admission to hospital, otherwise the detachment will progress.

63 Total retinal detachment in a patient who did not present himself until his visual loss was almost complete. The detachment had become total and the retina can be seen against the back of the lens in folds. There is a complete loss of the red reflex.

62

63

PART 4

Eye injuries

Minor eye injuries are extremely common; they range through superficial foreign bodies, traumatic ulcers, corrosive injuries, to the 'black eye'. Unfortunately, some major eye injuries of the globe or orbit may appear superficially like a 'black eye', while penetrating eye injuries may be completely misdiagnosed.

Minor eye injuries

Corneal foreign bodies   86

Subtarsal foreign bodies   92

Traumatic corneal ulcers   93

'Black eye' and associated major injuries (see below)   96

Major eye injuries

Closed injury   98
  Eye   98
  Orbit   108

Open injury   112

Minor injuries

Corneal foreign bodies

64 This patient states that something has blown into his eye. The visual acuity may be normal but there may be a considerable amount of lacrimation or photophobia. The foreign body can be seen slightly off-centre below and to the left of the pupil, immediately to the left of the large central highlight of the examiner's hand light. It must be removed, and after anaesthetising the cornea an attempt should be made to sweep it off with some cotton wool wrapped round an orange stick or a match stick.

65 Here an attempt is being made to sweep the foreign body off, but this is often unsuccessful.

66 The classical eye instrument for removing the corneal foreign body is a corneal spud. Here it is in use on an anaesthetised eye. As can be seen, it is flat but not sharp and therefore cannot do any untoward damage to the eye should the doctor or patient move involuntarily. The end is placed under the foreign body and it is flicked off the cornea.

67 The three instruments that may be used for removal of a foreign body. Uppermost is the classical corneal spud, which is easily used by those not experienced in ophthalmology, but is rather unwieldy and will cause a certain amount of superficial damage. Below that is the knife needle favoured by eye surgeons. This is extremely sharp and if used in unskilled hands can be thrust through the cornea. Below that is a commercially available orange stick with cotton wool wrapped around each end. This is ideal for attempting to sweep off a corneal foreign body. Below these are close-ups of the eye instruments themselves. A useful alternative that may be used in skilled hands is the sterile pre-packed disposable needle normally used on syringes. Whatever method is used to remove the foreign body, some epithelium will be lost as well, so that fluorescein must be placed in the eye to estimate the extent of epithelial loss.

68 Note the small green area at the site of the foreign body (same case as in **64**). The green area is pathognomonic of a **corneal ulcer** and all corneal ulcers should be treated by covering the eye.

69 If a metallic foreign body has been in the eye for more than a few hours, as it has been resting on a liquid medium it will rust and when it is removed a **rust ring** will remain behind. Note the circular brown ring, which is within the substance of the cornea — not on it. The removal of this will probably require expert assistance.

68

69

70

70 This patient complains of something in his eye. Careful examination shows the absence of a corneal foreign body or a foreign body in the lower or lateral fornices. In this type of case the lid should be everted as described in the method of examination. Here is seen the classical appearance of a foreign body in this situation. It should be removed with cotton wool or a handkerchief and the cornea subsequently stained with fluorescein to show any ulcer present.

71

71 A traumatic corneal ulcer. This patient complains of something in his eye. Examination should be done in this order:

a) Is there a corneal foreign body?

b) Is there a subtarsal foreign body?

c) If not, has the foreign body gone on to the eye, scratched it and come off again? Fluorescein will show this.

The eye should be covered with a pad and bandage to facilitate healing.

72

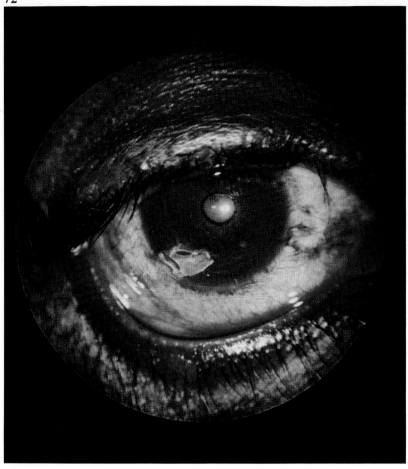

72 Burns with hot solid material should be assessed as in **71**. Fluorescein shows not only typical green areas of ulceration, but white coagulated material beneath them. These cases are best referred for specialist attention.

73 Corrosive burns caused by ammonia, as in this case, are diagnosed by fluorescein and then referred for specialist treatment. If the raw areas on the cornea and conjunctiva are opposite similar raw areas on the back of the lids, the two may fuse together. Treatment is immediate lavage with copious amounts of water. Do not wait for suitable neutralising agents, but plunge the patient's head under a tap or into a fire bucket, or any other nearby source of water.

'Black eye'

74 This is the typical '**black eye**', which can be defined as a lid haematoma. It is classically caused by a blunt injury to the orbit. However, all cases of black eye should be assessed with two things in mind:

a) Is the eye intact? Has there been a concussion injury to the eye? (**76–83**.)

b) Has there been a concussion injury to the orbit? (**84–86**.)

In such a case as depicted here it may be impossible to see the eye, but in a surprisingly short time the swelling will regress.

75 A black eye after the swelling has regressed. Note the haematoma of the lid and the sub-conjunctival haemorrhage, but note also that the cornea is bright and the pupil is round and central with a red reflex showing through. Clearly there is no intra-ocular damage.

74

75

Major eye injuries (closed)

76 Blood in the anterior chamber or a **hyphaema.** This classically follows a contusion injury to the eye and may present with the external physical signs of a black eye. Note that the blood is floating around in the anterior chamber and a level can be seen below. These will be the physical signs seen soon after the injury.

77 A classical hyphaema after the blood has been allowed to settle. There is an associated traumatic dilation of the pupil (mydriasis). In these cases the eye has received a severe injury, which takes it out of the category of a simple black eye into the category of a severe eye injury.

76

77

78 Rupture of the globe. The blow here has caused a hyphaema and has split the coats of the eye concentric with the limbus as shown by the dark swelling to one side. This again is obviously a severe injury.

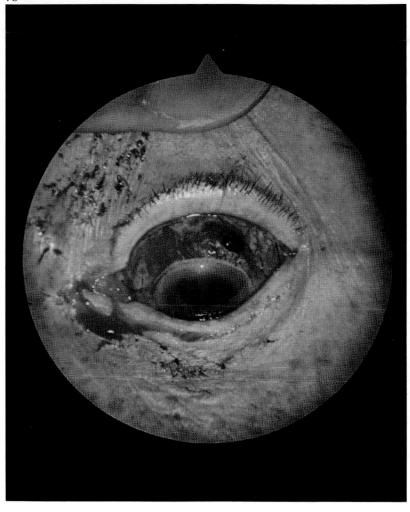

79 In this case the pressure wave generated by the blow on the front of the eye has passed from the back of the cornea and struck the iris, perhaps causing a hyphaema in the early stage, but also causing a tear of the root of the iris from its insertion, a so-called **iridodialysis.**

80 Concussion cataract and injury to the iris caused by a blow on the eye, the pressure wave striking the iris and the lens.

81 Oedema of the retina or **commotio retinae.** This may present as a simple black eye; the front of the eye appears clear, but at the back of the eye can be seen loss of red reflex around the inferior temporal vessels. Note the patch of white speckling, which may in severe cases become confluent. The white areas are caused by retinal thickening caused by the blow on the front of the eye.

82 In this case a blunt blow to the eye dislocated the lens, the curved edge of which can be seen within the dilated pupil. Other causes of dislocated lenses are hypermaturity or spontaneous dislocation, as in homocystinuria, or with arachnodactyly in Marfan's syndrome.

83 Choroidal rupture. In these cases the pressure wave is greater than in previous examples, and it strikes the back of the eye, severing the retina and the choroid. There may be retinal haemorrhages, as seen here, the white areas being the splits in the choroid with the sclera showing through.

Major orbital injuries

84 Blow-out fracture of the orbit. These cases may also appear as simple black eyes, and may have any of the contusion injuries of the globe itself. The pressure wave generated within the orbit strikes the orbital walls and fractures this where it is weakest and most unsupported, i.e. the floor (the roof of the maxillary sinus). A variable amount of the contents of the lower part of the orbit is incarcerated in the roof of the maxillary sinus. There is thus:

a) Enophthalmos.

b) Anaesthesia of the infra-orbital nerve.

c) Vertical double vision.

85 The patient is now attempting to look up. Notice that the gap between the lids and the limbus is greater on the left eye than the right, i.e. the right eye is not moving up as the muscles are incarcerated in the fracture of the floor of the orbit.

84

85

86 X-ray to show the little hernial sac, i.e. some of the contents of the orbit displaced down into the maxillary antrum. Thus all cases of black eye should be examined not only for injury to the eye but also for the integrity of the orbit.

Major eye injuries (open)

87 Penetrating eye injury. The patient classically states one of two things: a) he was using a hammer and chisel on concrete; or b) he was using a grindstone without goggles. In each case a small piece of metal flies backwards, perhaps travelling at several hundred miles an hour, and passes into the eye. As the coats of the eye are severed, and as the pressure inside the eye is higher than that of the atmosphere, there is a tendency for the intra-ocular contents to prolapse. If the penetration is anterior, this is characterised by an **iris prolapse,** which is the knuckle of pigment seen on the side of the limbus associated with **distortion of the pupil,** as some of the iris forming the border of the pupil is outside the eye. Such cases should be admitted immediately, as anything that raises the intra-ocular pressure may cause further prolapse of eye contents.

88 Traumatic cataract. The foreign body may strike the lens, rendering it opaque within a matter of hours. This makes subsequent visualisation and removal very difficult.

87

88

89 Multiple lacerations of the face and lids. These are very common following windscreen injuries and bottle fights. Such cases should be examined carefully, particularly in respect of the lacerations involving the lid margins. If they are involved they are probably best sutured by an eye surgeon, particularly those on the medial side, as they may well have involved the lower canaliculus — in which case immediate surgery is needed. All these cases should be examined for lacerations of the globe.

90 The same case as in **89**. When the swelling had reduced, it was possible to examine the globe carefully: a doubtful area on the temporal side can be seen.

89

90

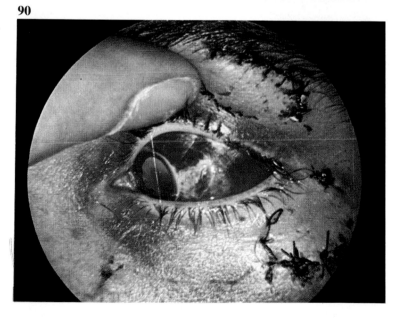

91 Close-up of the doubtful area in **90**, which shows an obvious full-thickness laceration requiring urgent attention.

92 & 92a All cases of injury to the upper eyelid should be examined with caution. In this case an apparently superficial injury well away from the lid margin was associated with a contusion injury in the globe manifesting itself as a hyphaema (see **77**). Such patients should be examined thoroughly, as the blunt foreign body may have damaged or penetrated the orbital plate of the frontal bone and produced central nervous system damage, e.g. injury with the point of an umbrella.

92

92a

93

93 This shows apparently superficial lacerations of the upper eyelid, but close examination of the globe demonstrates a pigmented cystic lesion at 7 o'clock on the limbus, which is an iris prolapse pathognomonic of a penetrating eye injury (see **87**).

PART 5

Miscellaneous eye conditions

Common conditions   122

This section includes common clinical conditions that do not otherwise fit into the clinical patterns previously described.

Less common conditions   146

After the conditions noted above there follows another collection of
miscellaneous pathological processes of less importance but all of
which show clear physical signs that are characteristic of their conditions and that can be easily seen using the method of examination
detailed previously.

Common miscellaneous conditions

Abnormalities of lid position

94 Note that this patient has a normal lid aperture on her left side, as shown by the limbus touching the lower lid and being overlapped by the upper one. Compare this with the aperture on the other side. Note that the limbus is separated from both lids by a white margin, thus in the upper lid there is **lid retraction** and from the lower lid it is obvious that the eye is being **pushed forwards.** This combination of lid retraction and/or proptosis can be very misleading.

95 A case of **thyrotoxicosis,** but note that there is bilateral symmetrical lid retraction and no proptosis, i.e. the limbus is just touched by the lower lids but there is a gap above.

94

95

96 A case of bilateral symmetrical lid retraction and proptosis, i.e. there is a gap between the limbus and lid above and below.

97 Note the enlarged vessels and rather swollen conjunctiva, which may be seen in the lateral fornices in thyrotoxicosis.

96

97

98 A case of bilateral symmetrical proptosis, i.e. a gap present between the limbus and the lower lids, but no lid retraction.

99 Entropion. The patient complains of a sore, running, red eye. On first examination conjunctivitis may be suspected, but a closer look shows that the lower lid is rolled over and the lashes are rubbing the eye. It is no use treating this condition with eye drops. The patient must be referred for minor surgery to turn the lid over. This condition is very commonly seen in old people.

100 Entropion. A case similar to **99**, but less obvious.

101 Ectropion. In these old people the lower lid loses its tone and drops away from the globe, particularly on the medial side. In these cases patients complain of a running eye as tears cannot drain down the passages. The primary cause is the lid position and this must be treated to restore continuity of the tear flow and drainage.

100

101

129

102 Ectropion. Another case showing how easily the condition can be missed. Note that the lower lid has fallen slightly away from the globe on the inner side.

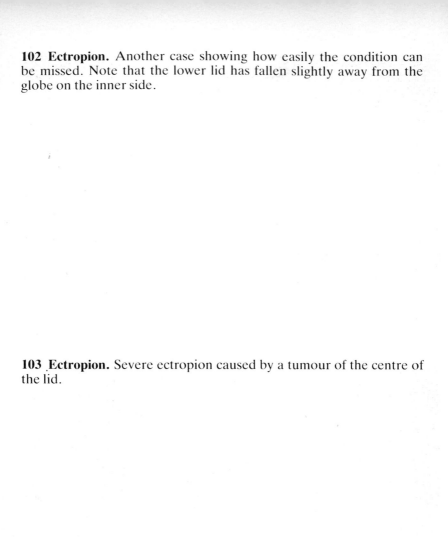

103 Ectropion. Severe ectropion caused by a tumour of the centre of the lid.

102

103

Pathology of the lids

104 Stye. The patient complains of a sore, swollen lid of a few days' duration. On examination there is a tender inflammatory swelling; on close inspection it is seen to be pointing round a lash follicle. Thus a stye can be defined as an acute infective process involving the lash follicles. It should be encouraged to point with 'hot spoon bathings' and treated with an antibiotic ointment to prevent a secondary conjunctivitis. Once it has pointed the offending lash should be removed.

105 Infected meibomian cyst. This patient also presents with a sore, swollen eyelid; it is infective, but close inspection shows that it is not pointing around the lashes, i.e. it is not a stye, but occurs above the lash line, at the junction of the inner and middle thirds in this case. It should be treated in the same way as a stye, but the patient should be told that once it has settled there will be a residual nodule present, which will almost certainly need incision and curettage.

104

105

106 A **meibomian cyst,** which may or may not become infected like the previous figure, in which case it may be confused with a stye.

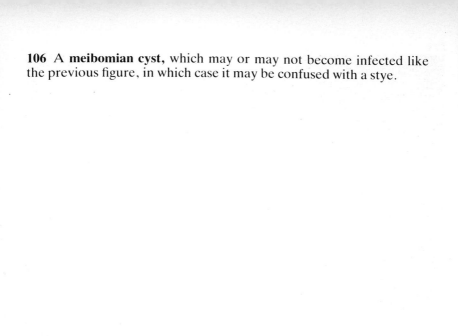

107 Two **meibomian cysts,** which appear as granulations on the glands of the deep surface of the lids. They may be seen by everting the appropriate lid.

106

107

108 A **basal cell carcinoma** or **rodent ulcer.** These are extremely common around the eyes. The diagnosis is made by the presence of a raised, pearly nodule, perhaps with a central ulcer. They are difficult to treat because both surgery and radiotherapy may cause complications.

Muscle pathology

109 Squint. A squint may be defined as a loss of parallelism of the visual axis. Ocular posture is a **reflex action,** thus any interference with this reflex may cause a squint. Thus a **sensory defect,** e.g. a corneal scar, a uniocular congenital cataract, or a uniocular retinal affliction, may cause a squint because there is no stimulus to keep the eye straight. Similarly, a **loss of the central fusion sense,** as is common in mentally deficient children, may also cause a squint. Interference on the **motor side,** that is a nerve palsy or a neuromuscular abnormality, or a congenital abnormality of the muscles themselves may cause a squint. In most ordinary cases the child is far-sighted and has to over-focus for distance, and consequently, while giving excessive accommodation for, say, reading, also shows excessive convergence and turns one eye in. The danger is that the eye that turns in may be suppressed and there may be a permanent loss of vision. Because of this, all squints should be seen promptly, as early treatment may restore binocular vision and because in rare cases there may be some disease causing the ocular deviation.

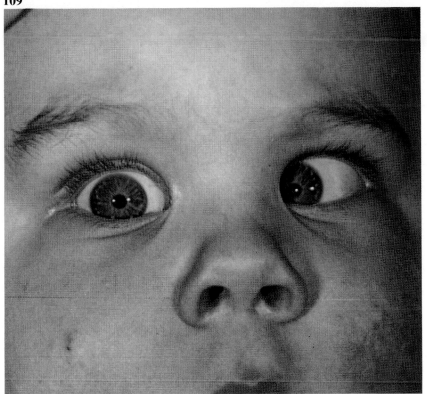

Disorders of lacrimal drainage

110 Epiphora, or a running eye. Diagram of the left tear passages showing that the tears may pass out over the globe, downwards and medially through the canaliculi into the lacrimal sac, through the lacrimal passages and into the nose. In a **newborn child,** the flap of membrane at the lower part of the tear passages may not canalise and the tears are dammed up. The baby has a continuously running eye, which intermittently becomes infected. Treatment is massage of the tear sac against the nasal bones, when in many cases the pressure may force the flap open. If this is not effective, probing may be necessary.

111 In **adults** there may be a chronic inflammatory stricture of the lower end of the tear sac and this may give an intermittent swelling near the inner canthus, as seen here, with a running eye.

112 An **abscess of the lacrimal sac** caused by infection of the stagnating tear sac contents (same case as **111**). Such cases are best referred for surgery.

111

112

Allergy

113 Allergy. This is becoming increasingly common and is particularly associated with penicillin or neomycin, and sometimes drops used in the treatment of glaucoma. The diagnosis is made by the appearance of a red eye with eczematous skin changes, as seen here. Clearly the drops must be stopped, but this may be difficult if the patient requires them for treatment of glaucoma. Such cases should be referred back to the eye surgeon.

Less common miscellaneous conditions

114 Xanthelasma, showing the characteristic raised, yellowish nodules situated within the skin. They may be larger and indeed confluent around the upper and lower lids of both eyes. They are said to indicate the presence of diabetes.

115 A lateral tarsorrhaphy. Note that the lids have been sutured together some time previously and the sutures removed. This manoeuvre is used in all cases where corneal cover is deficient, i.e. thyroid disease, any form of proptosis, VIIth nerve palsy, etc.

114

115

116 The appearance of multiple painless nodules within the skin of the lids of a member of the negro race should always suggest the diagnosis of **sarcoidosis,** which can easily be confirmed by biopsy of one of the lesions.

117 This is a **retention cyst** of one of the numerous glands on the edge of the lid. These are of no significance but are cosmetically unsatisfactory. They are easily treated by careful incision of the roof of the cyst and expression of the fatty contents.

118 Conjunctiva of the upper fornix. Note **mascara deposited sub-conjunctivally.** The upper lid has been everted and along its edge may be seen sub-conjunctival black patches caused by the deposition of mascara, which has been used for cosmetic purposes over some years. This condition is becoming increasingly common.

119 Vernal catarrh. The patient is usually young and complains of symptoms suggestive of conjunctivitis, but itching is a prominent symptom.

118

119

151

120 Argyrosis. This condition results from the deposition of silver following the use of silver nitrate drops over many years.

121 A spontaneous **sub-conjunctival haemorrhage.** These are common in middle-aged and elderly people and an isolated episode is of no significance. Further attacks may mean that there is a bleeding diathesis present.

120

121

122 A patch of **scleritis.** Note that the conjunctival congestion is only localised, but that there are also deeper vessels involved. Such a condition may be associated with systemic diseases, particularly of the arthritic type.

123 Scleromalacia. This is thinning of the sclera resulting from recurrent attacks of scleritis (see **122**).

124 Carotico-cavernous sinus fistula. The back pressure produces this tremendous dilation and congestion of the conjunctival veins, which is pathognomonic. In due course this congestion gives rise to raised intra-ocular pressure and the eye goes blind.

125 Pterygium. This is an extremely common fibro-vascular membrane, which may grow over the centre of the cornea. If it does so, it should be removed, as it may impede vision.

124

125

126 A **dermoid tumour,** seen in its characteristic position straddling the limbus. It is yellowish and raised. It should be removed.

127 A conjunctival **papilloma.** These may become very large and pedunculated, in which case they should be excised. They can be caused by a viral infection, in which case they may be multiple and extremely difficult to treat.

126

127

128 A lymphoma. The characteristic salmon pink swelling may occur in either the upper or lower fornix. Biopsy confirms the diagnosis, and although these lesions melt away with radiotherapy they may be associated with diffuse lymphomatous lesions elsewhere, or in the other orbit.

129 Arcus senilis. This is a deposition of fat just within the limbus, within the substance of the cornea. It is very common in middle-aged and old people and is of no significance.

128

129

130 Mustard gas keratitis. This is usually bilateral, can be associated with much scarring, and is characterised by the intra-corneal haemorrhages seen here.

131 A corneal graft that has failed because of a host–donor reaction. The circular scar at the bed of the donor may be seen, together with the stitch marks and the haze involving both.

132 A corneal contact lens. The curved border of the lens can be seen slightly offset from the limbus. There are white fibrous patches behind an irregular pupil, as this is a case of a traumatic cataract that has been partially removed in a young person. Binocular vision can be restored only by a contact lens or an intra-ocular plastic lens (see **133**). Tremendous advances have recently been made in contact lenses and intra-ocular plastic lenses, and there are very many types of both sorts. From the general point of view, it is worth remembering that some sorts of soft lenses can be ruined by the absorption of eye drops and, with the intra-ocular lenses, one must be very careful with regard to the application of drops that alter the size of the pupil. Both these problems are probably best dealt with by specialists.

133 An intra-ocular plastic lens can be seen in the anterior chamber. It has three limbs, two of which can be seen: one pointing outwards, the other downwards. This is also a case of a traumatic cataract, and two small holes in the iris can be seen.

132

133

134 An **aphakic eye,** i.e. one that has had the cataract removed, showing the common surgical end-result. Note that there is a clear black pupil and a small black segment at the periphery of the iris, which is an iridectomy, a manoeuvre always done when the lens is being removed surgically.

135 An **after-cataract.** Older techniques of cataract removal meant leaving behind the capsule of the lens, which occasionally thickened, giving an appearance like this. In these cases vision can be restored only by further minor operation.

136 Rubeosis of the iris in a diabetic. Note that the pupil is off-centre, the iris atrophic and covered by a sheet of fine blood vessels. This is often the end-result of diabetes affecting the eye.

137 Coloboma of the iris. Note that the iris is deficient downwards. This is a congenital defect caused by faulty closure of the optic vesicle. It is frequently associated with similar defects in the retina and choroid (see **140**).

138 A malignant melanoma of the iris and ciliary body. Note that there is a dark swelling pushing forward from the iris and is clearly arising from its root. Such a tumour, if left, will spread round the angle of the eye and give a form of glaucoma.

137

138

139 An **endophthalmitis.** Note that the eye is congested, the pupil irregular as a result of iridocyclitis and there is a yellowish reflex (pus) from the back. This may be seen in cases of septicaemia, when the eye virtually becomes a bag of pus.

140 A **choroidal coloboma.** This is a congenital malformation of the choroid and retina often seen with an iris coloboma (see **137**). The normal retina and choroid is seen on one side, while in the pale area is a deficiency of these structures, the ophthalmoscope viewing the sclera directly.

139

140

141 Astroid hyalitis. This is a benign, symptomless degeneration of the vitreous, characterised by minute yellowish balls floating within the eye and easily seen with the ophthalmoscope. Although very dramatic, they are of no significance. They should be distinguished from synchysis scintillans, which appears only on movement of the eye and is characterised by the appearance of 'small burnished plates', which disappear again when the eye moves back to its original position. This condition is also of no significance, but is sometimes worrying to the examining clinician.

142 Myelinated nerve fibres. This condition causes undue worry, but is of no significance as it is symptom-free and is merely the prolongation into the eye of the myelination process that occurs in the CNS. It should be noted and explained to the patient merely to prevent anxiety in the future.

141

142

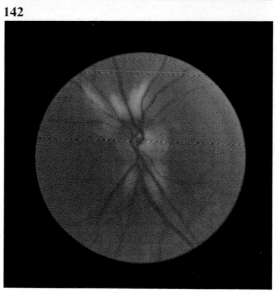

143 A squint. Note that the left eye of the patient is convergent but that there is also a white reflex. This is pathognomonic of a **retinoblastoma** — a tumour that may be hereditary and may involve both eyes of a child. (Compare with **109**.)

144 A naevus of the choroid. A darkly pigmented patch occurring at the back of the eye. These require continued observation as they may become malignant and give rise to a malignant melanoma of the choroid.

143

144

145 Metastasis in the choroid. Two ill-defined, yellow, slightly raised patches occurring in the eye of a woman dying from metastases. These are frequently larger and are probably more common than is suspected.

146 Retinal folds. These can be seen traversing the back of the eye, spreading from the optic disc across the macula. In many cases they are caused by pressure outside the eye from a tumour, or, rarely, in thyroid disease.

145

146

147 A retinal angioma. The tumour can be seen between the feeding artery and the draining vein. Retinal angiomata may enlarge and cause visual loss but are easily treated at this stage. It must not be forgotten that they may be associated with angiomata elsewhere, particularly as part of a von Hippel–Lindau syndrome, when the CNS may be involved.

Index

**References are to figure numbers,
not page numbers.**

Acute conjunctivitis **28 & 29**
Acute glaucoma **33–35**
After-cataract **135**
Allergy **113**
Angioma, of retina **147**
Aperture of lids **94**
Aphakic eye **134**
Application of fluorescein **7**
Aqueous humour, flow of **35**
Arcuate scotoma in glaucoma **58**
Arcus senilis **129**
Argyrosis **120**
Arteritis, giant cell or temporal **60**
Astroid hyalitis **141**
Atrophy of the optic nerve **59**
Atrophy of the optic nerve — glaucomatous **57**

Basal cell carcinoma of lid **108**
Black eye **74–86**
Blepharitis **27**
Blood in anterior chamber (hyphaema) **76 & 77**
Blow-out fracture **84–86**
Burns **72 & 73**

Carotico-cavernous sinus fistula **124**
Cataract **40–45**
 –concussion **76**
 –traumatic **88**
Central fields **24–26**
Choroidal rupture **83**
Choroido-retinitis **52 & 53**
Coloboma
 –of choroid **140**
 –of iris **137**
Commotio retinae **81**
Conjunctivitis **28 & 29**
Corneal foreign bodies **64–69**
Corneal graft (failed) **131**
Corneal oedema **33**
Corneal reflex **3**
Corneal rust ring **69**
Corneal ulcers
 –non-traumatic **36 & 37**
 –traumatic **71–73**

Cyst of lid **105–107, 117**
Cyst, meibomian **105–107**

Dendritic ulcer **36 & 37**
Dermoid **126**
Diabetic retinopathy **48, 50 & 51**
Dislocated lens **82**

Ectropion **101–103**
Endophthalmitis **139**
Entropion **99 & 100**
Epiphora **110**
Eversion of lid **5 & 6**
Examination of:
 –outside of eye **3 & 4**
 –inside of eye **10–16**
 –intra-ocular pressure **17–19**
 –tear passages **20**
 –visual acuity **1 & 2**
 –visual fields **21–26**

Fluorescein, application of **7**
Foreign body
 –corneal **64–69**
 –intra-ocular **87**
 –subtarsal **70**
Fracture, blow-out **84–86**
Fundus of eye **14–16**

Giant cell arteritis **60**
Glaucoma
 –acute **33–35**
 –chronic **57 & 58**
 –fields (chronic) **58**
 –optic disc (chronic) **57**

Haemorrhage, sub-conjunctival **121**
Hand light, to examine outside of eye **3 & 4**
Hemianopia **24**
Herpes simplex **37**
Herpes zoster **39**
Hypertensive retinopathy **46 & 47**
Hyphaema **76 & 77**
Hypopyon ulcer **38**

Intra-ocular lens 133
Intra-ocular pressure 17–19
–acute rise 33–35
–chronic rise 57 & 58
Iridocyclitis 30–32
Iridodialysis 79
Iris coloboma 137
Iris prolapse 87, 93
Iris rubeosis 136

Keratic precipitates 31 & 32
Keratitis, mustard gas 130

Lacerations, multiple 89–93
Lacrimal disorders 110–112
Lid aperture
–normal 94
–changes 94–98
Lid cyst 105–107, 117
Lid margin, inflammation (blepharitis) 27
Lid position changes 99–103
Light coagulation in diabetic retinopathy
50 & 51
Limbus, definition of 28
Lymphoma 128

Malignant melanoma 138
Meibomian cyst 105–107
Metastases of the choroid 145
Myelinated nerve fibres 142

Naevus of choroid 144

Oedema of conjunctiva 97
Oedema of cornea 33
Ophthalmoscope, use of 10–13
Optic disc
–cupping 57
–normal 14
–swelling 54–56
Orbit, blow-out fracture of 84–86

Papilloedema 54–56
Papilloma
–conjunctival 127
Penetrating injury of eye 87–93
Peripheral fields 21–26
Posterior synechiae 31
Pressure, intra-ocular
–estimation of 17–19
–increase of (acute) 33
–increase of (chronic) 57 & 58
Prolapse of iris 87
Proptosis 96–98
Pterygium 125

Pupil
–in acute glaucoma 33
–in iridocyclitis 31
–in penetrating injury 87

Red reflex 11
Retention cyst 117
Retinal angioma 147
Retinal artery block 60
Retinal detachment 62 & 63
Retinal folds 146
Retinal oedema (traumatic) 81
Retinal vein block 61
Retinoblastoma 143
Retinopathy
–diabetic 48, 50 & 51
–hypertensive 46 & 47
Retraction of lids 94 & 95
Rodent ulcer 108
Rupture of choroid 83
Rupture of globe 78

Sarcoidosis 116
Scleritis 122
Scleromalacia 123
Scotoma
–arcuate 58
–central 24
Shingles 39
Slit-lamp 8 & 9
Snellen test chart 1
Squint 109
Steroid cataract 45
Steroid drops 32 & 38
Stye 104
Sub-conjunctival haemorrhage 121
Syphilitic choroido-retinitis 53

Tarsorrhaphy 115
Temporal arteritis 60
Thyrotoxicosis 94–98
Tonometer
–applanation 19
–Schiøtz 18
Toxoplasmosis 52

Ulcers, corneal
–non-traumatic 36 & 37
–traumatic 71–73
Ulcers, dendritic 36 & 37
Ulcers, hypopyon 38

Vernal catarrh 119
Visual acuity 1 & 2

Xanthelasma 114